The Teachers of the Training Department (Grades 1-8) of the Los Angeles State Normal School, encouraged and otherwise assisted by the President of the School, the Supervisor of the Training School, and Teachers of English and Reading, present this booklet, dedicated to

Service

Preface

To serve the children in our Training School, the students in our Normal School, and children and teachers generally, is the mission of this booklet.

The literature referred to is the best that we can suggest. When better shall come to our attention, that will be included, for only "the best is good enough for children." The blank pages in the booklet may serve for additions and notes. All selections presented have been tried either in this school or elsewhere. Nothing is presented wholly on a theoretical basis. Much literature is offered for each grade—much more than can possibly be presented. The intention is to refer to types of suitable material, leaving to the teacher the selection of that which best accords with the characteristics of the pupils and the limitations of the school library. Sometimes the teacher will find the material that will best suit the pupils in a list several grades either above or below the one indicated. This is true, both of the school work and of the home reading.

Considered in a large way, the titles suggested indicate the "content side" of our literature course for the grades. Search on this side will not, however, reveal progressive continuity in thought, nor a center of correlation, nor a correspondence with racial development. Those selections which seem best to accord with the general or specific needs of the pupils, those which express something that is vital to the pupils, those which put in good form the unformed or half-formed ideals of the pupils, those which present advanced ideals to the pupils, ideals of both content and form, always those which are enjoyable to the pupils at the same time appealing to their developing æsthetic appreciation—those are the selections made. Occasional repetitions may be noted even in successive grades. Children do not change so much in a half year or even in a whole year as to make a certain selection fit to be given at only one of those times. Neither do we fear occasionally to repeat a selection with no more than one year intervening. Children often do not get all there is, even for them, in a selection at its first presentation. Besides, the method of approach may be varied when the selection is repeated, so that pupils may often, for example, greet an old friend when they, in a higher grade, read the selection that was read to them earlier, or even still earlier told to them. The methods of approach that are indicated as suitable are intended to be suggestive only. Parts of many selections which are considered suitable, for example, to be read by the children, might well be read to them and still other parts told to them. There is no intention of giving a prescription either as to material or to method.

A select list of references on the pedagogy of literature is given. The importance of the telling of stories and of dramatization is recognized by reference lists on these topics. One play (the first one presented in the Intermediate Grades in the Training School, in which the text was worked out chiefly by the pupils under teacher direction) is published. A few illustrations follow, showing how with only slight suggestions in the way of costume and with no stage accessories, dramatizations have been given.

In story telling and dramatization, as in most other things, little children are leading us to the "everlasting better."

EVERETT SHEPARDSON,

. Supervisor Training School.

Los Angeles State Normal School,

    June 23, 1908.

Table of Contents

Keys

The small letters used at the left of most titles have the following significance:

a—Suitable to be **told to** children.
b—Suitable to be **read to** children.
c—Suitable to be **read by** children.
d—Suitable, as a whole or in part, to be **dramatized.**
e—Suitable, as a whole or in part, for **memorizing.**

When figures are used at the right of titles, they refer to where the selections may be found as designated in the first succeeding list of sources.

First Grade

BEATRICE CHANDLER PATTON, Training Teacher

FABLES

a, d.	The Lion and the Mouse - - Scudder, also in 5.
a, d.	Belling the Cat - - Scudder, also in 5.
a, d.	The Crow and the Pitcher - - Scudder, also in 5.
a, d.	The Town Mouse and the Country Mouse - - Heart of Oak, II., also in 2, 5, 7.
a, d.	The Lark and the Farmer - - Heart of Oak, II., also in 7, 2, 5.
a, d.	Wolf! Wolf! - - Æsop, also in 7, 2.
a, d.	The Wind and the Sun - - Sara Cone Bryant, also in 7, 2, 5.
a, d.	The Hare and the Tortoise - - Scudder, also in 5.

NURSERY TALES

a, d.	Stories from Mother Goose - - Heart of Oak, I.
a, b.	Mother Goose Village - - Madge Bigham.

CONSTRUCTIVE STORIES

a, d.	The Little Red Hen - - Baker and Carpenter, also in 6.
a.	The Old Woman and Her Pig - - Baker and Carpenter, also in 6.
a.	Titty Mouse and Tatty Mouse - - Baker and Carpenter.
a.	The Gingerbread Man - - Sara Cone Bryant.
a.	The Pancake Story - - Dasent.
a.	Henny Penny - - Dasent, also in 2.
a.	Who Killed the Otter's Babies? - - Sara Cone Bryant.

FAIRY TALES

a, d, b.   Cinderella - - Perrault, also in 2, 4, 17.

a and b.   East of the Sun and West of the Moon - - Dasent; or, the same

a.   as Beauty and the Beast (adapted) - - Scudder, also in 15, 17.

a.   Hop o' My Thumb - - Perrault, also in 2.

a.   Faithful John - - Grimm.

a.   The Fisherman and His Wife - - Grimm, also in 2.

a, d.   Little Red Riding Hood - - Heart of Oak, II., also in 2, 17.

a, d, b.   Hansel and Grethel - - Grimm, also in 17.

a.   The House in the Wood - - Grimm.

a, d.   The Pig that Set up Housekeeping - - Dasent.

b and a, d.   Briar Rose - - Grimm, also in 2, 6, 17.

a, d.   The Three Pigs - - Baldwin.

a.   Peter, Paul, and Espen - - Dasent.

d, a.   The Three Billy Goats Gruff - - Dasent, also in 11.

a, b.   The Adventures of the Little Field Mouse - - Sara Cone Bryant.

a, d.   Little One Eye - - Grimm, also in 2.

a.   Rumple-Stilts-Kin - - Grimm.

a, d.   Snow White and Rose Red - - Grimm.

a, d.   The Three Bears - - Heart of Oak, II., also in 2, 6.

a, d.   The Wolf and the Seven Goats - - Grimm.

a, d.   The Shoemaker and the Elves - - Sara Cone Bryant, also in 12, 2.

b and a, d.   The Woodman and the Goblins - - Elementary School Teacher, April, 1904.

a.   The Wren and the Bear - - Grimm.

a, d.   The Frog Prince - - Grimm, also in 2.

HUMOROUS TALES

b.   The Tale of Peter Rabbit - - Beatrice Potter.

a, b.   The Tar Baby - - Uncle Remus, Harris.

b.   Goops and How to be Them - - G. Burgess.

b.   Little Black Sambo - - Warne Co., New York.
b, a.   The Story of Epaminondas - - Sara Cone Bryant.
b, a.   The Little Jackal and the Alligator - - Sara
          Cone Bryant.
b, a.   The Talkative Tortoise - - Sara Cone Bryant.
a, d.   Bremen Town Musicians - - Grimm, also in 2.
a.   The Cat and the Parrot - - Sara Cone Bryant.

SELECTIONS FROM

a and b. Peter Pan - - J. M. Barrie.
a, b.   Lady Hollyhock and Her Friends - - M. E.
          Walker.

HERO STORIES

a.   Daniel in the Lions' Den - - The Bible, also in 7.
a.   David and Goliath - - The Bible, also in 7.
a.   St. George and the Dragon - - Chenoweth.
a.   Little Hero of Haarlem - - Sara Cone Bryant.

STORIES OF INDUSTRY

a.   (Adapted) Life of Lucca Della Robbia - - Va-
          sari's Lives of the Painters, Vol. II.
a.   (Adapted) Life of Palissy, the Potter - - Pub.
          by Ira Bradley Co., Boston.
a.   Stories of the Lives of Firemen, Fishermen, Lum-
          bermen, etc.

ANIMAL STORIES

a.   The Elephant's Child - - Just So Stories, Kip-
          ling.
a, b.   How the Camel Got His Hump - - Just So
          Stories, Kipling.
a, b.   How the Rhinoceros Got His Skin - - Just So
          Stories, Kipling.
a, b.   How the Whale Got His Throat - - Just So
          Stories, Kipling.
b, a.   The White Seal - - Jungle Book, Kipling.
b, a.   Her Majesty's Servant - - Jungle Book, Kip-
          ling.

b, a.   Toomaii of the Elephants - - Jungle Book, Kipling.

a.   (Selections from) Little Folks in Feathers and Fur - - O. Thorne Miller.

a.   Little Grey Pony - - Mother Stories, Lindsay.

a.   Voices for the Speechless - - A. Firth.

b, a.   The Cave Man - - K. Dopp.

b, a.   The Tree Man - - K. Dopp.

a.   Animals, Wild and Tame - - Davis.

a and b.   Raggylug - - Ernest Thompson Seton.

a and b.   Animal Books - - E. Nister.

a.   Four Feet, Two Feet, No Feet - - Richards.

FOR TEACHERS

Our Feathered Friends - - Grinnell.

Bird Day - - C. A. Babcock.

Birds and Bees - - J. Burroughs.

Jingle Book of Birds - - E. B. Clark.

Our Common Birds - - J. B. Grant.

Short Stories of Shy Neighbors - - Mrs. M. A. Kelly.

In Nesting Time - - O. T. Miller.

Four Feet, Two Feet, No Feet - - Richards.

Wood Folk Series - - William Long.

Friends and Helpers - - Sarah Eddy.

INDIAN STORIES

a and b.   Zitkala-Sa, Indian Legends - - Pub. by Ginn & Co.

a and b.   Hiawatha, selected - - Longfellow.

a, b.   Zuñi Folk Tales - - Cushing.

a, b.   Wigwam Stories - - Judd.

a, b.   Stories of Indian Children - - Husted.

a.   The Eagle and the Linnet - - Elementary School Teacher, Vol 2.

a.   Weeng - - Elementary School Teacher, Vol. 2.

a.   The Guiding Star - - Elementary School Teacher, Vol. 2.

a.   The Star and the Lily - - Elementary School Teacher, Vol. 2.

a.   The Sun and the Rabbit   -   -   Elementary School
            Teacher, Vol. 2.

THANKSGIVING

The First Thanksgiving   -   -   Wiggin.
Thanksgiving Day   -   -   Open Sesame, Vol. I.
Jericho Bob   -   -   St. Nicholas, Vol. 19.
Merry Thought   -   -   St. Nicholas, Vol. 21.
Old Time Thanksgiving   -   -   St. Nicholas, Vol. 24, also Vol.
   9 (1882).
Wooly Coats' Thanksgiving   -   -   Child's Garden of Story
   and Song, November, 1901.

FOR TEACHERS

Holidays and Festivals   -   -   A. M. Earle.
How to Celebrate Thanksgiving   -   -   Kellog.
Thanksgiving Day Fancies   -   -   Scribner, Vol. 18 (1895).
Thanksgiving   -   -   Scribner, Vol. 9.
After Br'er Rabbit   -   -   Century, Vol. 53 (1896).
Thanksgiving Procession   -   -   Primary Education, Novem-
   ber, 1906.
The First Thanksgiving   -   -   Primary Education, Novem-
   ber, 1906.

ARBOR DAY—BIRD DAY

See Wisconsin Arbor and Bird Day Annual of 1902. This
   contains suggestive lists for reference and treats of—
The Tree Planters,
The Little Plant,
Do You Know the Trees by Name?
The Heart of the Tree,
The Secret,
The Little Brown Wren,
Nature's Miracle: Tree Planting,
Pine Needles,
Plant a Tree.

Holy Days and Holidays - - Deems, Compiler.
How to Celebrate Arbor Day in the Schoolroom - - Practical Teachers' Library, Vol. 3, No. 3.
Arbor Day Manual - - C. B. Skinner.
The Little Pine Tree - - St. Nicholas, Vol. 5.
Heart of the Tree - - Century, Vol. 45 (1892-3).
Three Trees - - St. Nicholas, Vol. 18 (1891).
Songs of Nature - - Burroughs.
Bare Boughs and Buds - - St. Nicholas, Vol. 18 (1891).
Tree Planting - - Songs of the Tree Top and Meadow.
Arbor Day - - Harris and Gilbert's Guide Books to English, Book I.
See also List for Teachers under Animal Stories.

MAY DAYS

The Flowers - - Dodge.
Signs of May - - When Life is Young, Dodge.
May Pole Dance - - St. Nicholas, Vol. 24 (1897).
May Day - - Harris and Gilbert's Guide Books to English, Book I.
Decoration Day Poems - - Farm Legends, W. Carleton.

HALLOWE'EN

Myths - - St. Nicholas, Vol. 9 (1881-2).
Witches' Night - - St. Nicholas, Vol. 6 (1878-9).
The Woodman and the Goblins - - Elementary School Teacher, April, 1904.

CHRISTMAS

Legend of Christmas - - In Storyland, E. Harrison.
Christmas Bells - - Arnold, St. Nicholas, Vol. 21.
The Mistletoe Bough - - Open Sesame, Vol. III.
Observations on Christmas Eve - - St. Nicholas, Vol. 23.
Christmas Day - - St. Nicholas, Vol. 6.
Little Christmas Spy - - St. Nicholas, Vol. 16.
Old Christmas - - Poetry for Children, Eliot.
Visiting Santa Claus - - St. Nicholas, Vol. 12.
Legend of St. Nicholas - - Harper's, Vol. 74.
Christmas Eve Thought - - St. Nicholas, Vol. 23.

The First Christmas Tree - - Profitable Tales, Field.
The Baby's Christmas - - Century, Vol. 25.
Christmas in England - - Scannell.
Christmas in France - - Scannell.
Christmas in Germany - - Scannell.
Christmas in Italy - - Scannell.
The Fir Tree - - Andersen.
Tiny Tim - - Dickens.
Christmas, Every Day - - Howells.
Five Minute Stories - - Richards.
A Christmas Legend - - St. Nicholas, Vol. 2.
Piccola - - Wiggin.
Gretchen - - In Storyland, E. Harrison.
Story of Christmas - - Story Hour, Wiggin.
Story of the Forest - - Story Hour, Wiggin.
Our Holidays - - Retold from St. Nicholas, 1905.
Book of Christmas - - T. K. Hervey.
Christmas Pantomimes - - St. Nicholas (1887-8).
City Legends - - Will Carleton.
For Christmas - - Celia Thaxter.
Bells of Christmas - - The Posy Ring, Wiggin and Smith.
Baucis and Philemon - - Classic Myths, Charles Mills
    Gayley.
Legend of Christmas - - December Plan Book.
Christmas in Other Lands - - Marian George.

EASTER

Herr Oster - - Hase.
Charcoal-Burners' Fire - - St. Nicholas, Vol. 5, p. 499.
Bulletin, Chicago Public Library - - Special Bulletin No. 3.
Easter Poem - - M. M. Dodge.
Easter Dawn - - Lucy Larcon.
Easter Morning - - Harper's, Vol. 56.
Song of Easter - - Celia Thaxter, St. Nicholas, Vol. 6.

POETRY

N. B.—To be READ TO children.

THE POSY RING—Kate Douglas Wiggin and Nora Archibald Smith.

Marjorie's Almanac.
In February.
Nearly Ready.
The Coming of Spring.
September.
How the Leaves Came Down.
e. Winter Night.
What the Winds Bring.
Lady Moon.
Now the Noisy Winds Are Still.
The Wind in a Frolic.
e. Guessing Song.
Who Stole the Bird's Nest?
e. The Bluebird.
e. What Does Little Birdie Say?
White Butterflies.
Little White Lily.
e. Baby Seed Song.
Baby Corn.
e. For Good Luck.
e. Thank You, Pretty Cow.
e. Wishing.
e. Birdies with Broken Wings.
Good-Night and Good-Morning.
The World's Music.
Little Gustava.
Deaf and Dumb.
The Fairy Folk.
A Fairy in Armor.
The Last Voyage of the Fairies.
The Child and the Fairies.
e. The Little Elf.
e. One, Two, Three.
Discontent.

e. Thanksgiving Day.
    A Thanksgiving Fable.
    The Owl and the Pussy Cat.
    The Fairies, Shopping.
    The Fairies of the Caldon-Low.
e. The Elf and the Dormouse.
    The Cow-boy's Song.
    Rockaby, Lullaby.
e. Sleep, My Treasure.
e. The Sandman.
    All Things Bright and Beautiful.
    A Child's Thought of God.
    Night and Day.
e. Why Do Bells of Christmas Ring?
e. A Visit from St. Nicholas.
    Santa Claus.

SING SONG—Christina Rosetti.

Pages 26, 41, 43, 44, 58, 60, 61, 66, 75, 81, 84, 77, 76, 86, 106, 107, 105.

A CHILD'S GARDEN OF VERSES—Robert Louis Stevenson.

e. Bed in Summer.
    At the Seaside.
    Whole Duty of Children.
e. Rain.
    The Land of Counterpane.
e. My Shadow.
    Marching Song.
    The Cow.
    The Wind.
    Foreign Children.
    The Sun's Travels.
e. The Moon.
e. The Swing.
e. Time to Rise.
    The Unseen Playmate
    Autumn Fires.
    Nest Eggs.

WITH TRUMPET AND DRUM—Eugene Field.
> The Sugar-Plum Tree.
> Little Blue Pigeon (Japanese Lullaby).
> Wynken, Blynken, and Nod (Dutch Lullaby).

LOVE SONGS OF CHILDHOOD—Eugene Field.
> e. The Rock-a-By Lady.
> The Night Wind.
> So, So, Rock-a-by So!
> The Duel.

SONGS OF THE TREE TOP AND MEADOW—Lida McMurry and Agnes Cook.
> September.
> Thistledown.
> The Fairies in Winter.
> e. Giving Thanks.
> e. Twinkle, Twinkle, Little Star.
> Singing.
> e. I Love You, Mother.
> e. I am the Family Cat.
> If I Knew.
> The Indian Mother's Lullaby.
> Lullaby of the Iroquois.
> Two Wise Owls.
> e. Tree Planting.
> e. At Easter Time.
> Strength.
> e. The Flag Goes By.
> e. The Baby.
> Sleep, Baby, Sleep.
> e. April.
> Calling the Violet.
> e. Clovers.
> Remorse.
> The Song of the Lilies.
> e. The Secret.
> e. The Seed.
> Somebody's Knocking.
> e. A Child's Answer.
> Daisies and Buttercups.

GUIDE BOOKS TO ENGLISH, BOOK I.—Harris and Gilbert.

I'll Try.
' Three Bugs.
"I'll Shine," Says the Sun.
The Clucking Hen.   .
e. The Flag.
Cradle Songs.
The Fox and the Cat.
Wise Sayings.

OTHER POETRY

Ariel's Song - - In 17.
Song of the Fairy - - Midsummer Night's Dream, also in 17.
The Fairies - - In 17.
The Lamb - - Blake, in Heart of Oak, II.
Over in the Meadow - - In Heart of Oak, II.

SOURCES

1. Sir George Dasent: Popular Tales from the Norse, Putnam's Sons, New York.
2. Horace E. Scudder: Fables and Folk Stories, Houghton, Mifflin Co.
3. Grimm, edited by J. M. Dent, London, Trans. by Mrs. E. Lucas; edited also by E. P. Dutton, New York.
4. Hans Christian Andersen - - Rand, McNally.
5. Æsop.
6. Heart of Oak Books, Second Book, edited by Charles Eliot Norton.
7. Sara Cone Bryant: Stories to Tell to Children, Houghton, Mifflin Co.
8. Elizabeth Harrison: In Storyland, Sigma Publishing Co., Chicago.
9. Mary Mapes Dodge: Rhymes and Jingles.
10. Mary Mapes Dodge: When Life is Young.
11. Baker and Carpenter: First Year Language Reader, Macmillan Co.
12. James L. Baldwin: Fairy Stories and Fables.
13. The Elementary School Teacher.

14. Sara Cone Bryant: How to Tell Stories to Children.
15. Andrew Lang: Blue Fairy Book, A. L. Burt Co., New York.
16. Henry W. Longfellow: Hiawatha.
17. Laura Winmington: The Outlook Fairy Book, The Outlook Co.
18. Tales of Mother Goose, edited by M. V. O'Shea, Heath Co.

Second and B-Third Grades

HELEN C. MACKENZIE, Training Teacher

FAIRY TALES
B2 Grade

a.   Aladdin - - Scudder, also in 4.
a, d. Cinderella - - Scudder, also in 4.
a, d. The Frog Prince - - Scudder, also in 1.
a.   The Golden Goose - - Grimm, also in 4.
a.   Hop o' My Thumb - - Scudder.
a.   Jack and the Bean Stalk - - Scudder.
a.   The Three Billy Goats Gruff - - Dasent.
a.   Tom Thumb - - Grimm, also in 4.
a, d. The Wolf and the Seven Kids - - Grimm.

A2 Grade

a.   Beauty and the Beast - - Scudder, also in 4.
a.   Clever Alice - - Grimm, also in 3.
a.   Jack, the Giant Killer - - Lang.
a, d. The Sleeping Beauty - - Grimm, also in 3.
a.   One Eye, Two Eyes, Three Eyes - - Grimm, also in 3.
a, d. Toads and Diamonds - - Lang.
a.   The Storks - - Andersen.
a.   The Ugly Duckling - - Andersen, also in 3.
a, d. Snow White and Rose Red - - Grimm, also in 4.
a.   Little Ida's Flowers - - Andersen.
a.   Whittington and His Cat - - Lang.

SOURCES

1. Grimm: Tales, translated by Mrs. Lucas.
2. Andersen: Tales, translated by Mrs. Lucas.
3. Scudder: The Children's Book.
4. Lang: Blue Fairy Book.
5. Dasent: Popular Tales from the Norse.

GREEK MYTHS

B2 Grade

a. Arachne - - Baldwin, also in 4.
a. Clytie and the Sun God - - Firth, also in 5.
a. Contest between Apollo and Pan - - Francillon, also in 6.
a. Echo and Narcissus - - Francillon, also in 6.
a. Latona and the Frogs - - Kupfer.
a. Phaethon - - Firth, also in 5.

A2 Grade

a. Apples of Hesperides - - The Wonder Book, also in 5.
a. The Chimera - - The Wonder Book.
a, d. The Golden Touch - - The Wonder Book, also in 5.
a. Pandora - - The Wonder Book, also in 4, 5.
a. The Pigmies - - Tanglewood Tales.

B3 Grade

a. Admetus - - Kupfer.
a. Atalanta - - Baldwin.
a. Ceres and Persephone - - Tanglewood Tales, also in 5, 6.
a. Circe's Palace - - Tanglewood Tales.
a. The Dragon's Teeth - - Tanglewood Tales, also in 3.
a. The Gorgon's Head - - Firth, also in 5, 6.
a. Prometheus - - Firth, also in 3.
a. Theseus and the Minotaur - - Francillon, also in 6.
a. The Wonderful Artisan - - Francillon, also in 6.

SOURCES

1. Hawthorne: The Wonder Book.
2. Hawthorne: Tanglewood Tales.
3. Baldwin: Old Greek Stories.
4. Firth: Stories of Old Greece.
5. Francillon: Gods and Heroes.
6. Kupfer: Stories of Long Ago.

NORSE MYTHOLOGY
B3 Grade

a.   Iduna's Apples - - Stearn, also in 2, 3, 4.
a.   Sif's Hair - - Baldwin, also in 4, 5 (second year).
a.   Freya's Necklace - - Keary.
a.   Thor and the Frost Giant - - Stearn, also in 2, 5 (fifth year).
a.   How Thor Went Fishing - - Keary.
a.   The Death of Baldur - - Keary, also in 4, 5 (fifth year).
a.   The Forging of the Sword - - Baldwin, also in 5 (fifth year).
a.   The Choosing of Gram - - Baldwin, also in 4, 5 (fifth year).
a.   The Slaying of the Dragon - - Baldwin, also in 4.

SOURCES

1.   Stearn: The Gods of Our Fathers.
2.   Keary: The Heroes of Asgard.
3.   Baldwin: The Story of Siegfried. ·
4.   Guerber: Myths of Northern Lands.
5.   Baker and Carpenter: Language Readers (fifth year and second year).

IN STORYLAND—Elizabeth Harrison.
B2 Grade

a.   Prince Harweda.
a.   The Cabbage Butterfly.
a.   The Line of Golden Light.

A2 Grade

a.   The Mill Window.
a.   Beta and the Lame Giant.
a.   The Wonderful Sea God.

B3 Grade

a.   The Line of Golden Light.
a.   How Cedric Became a Knight.
a.   Columbus.

ORGANIC EDUCATION—Harriet M. Scott.
B2 Grade
a.   Hiawatha, the Indian Boy.
a.   Kablu, the Aryan Boy.

A2 Grade
a.   Darius, the Persian Boy.
a.   Cleon, the Greek Boy.

B3 Grade
a.   Horatius, the Roman Boy.
a.   Wulf, the Saxon Boy.

IN THE CHILD'S WORLD—Emily Poulsson.

BIBLE STORIES
B2 Grade
a.   Joseph.
a.   Jacob.

A2 Grade
a.   Samson.
a.   Daniel.

B3 Grade
a.   David.
a.   Abraham.
a.   Jacob.
a.   Moses.

MOTHER STORIES—Maud Lindsay.

B2 Grade

a. Giant Energy and Fairy Skill.
a. The Search for a Good Child.
a. Dust Under the Rug.
a. Story of Gretchen (Christmas).

THE STORY HOUR—Kate Douglas Wiggin.

A2 Grade

a. Dick Smiley's Birthday.
a. Benjamin in Beastland.
a. The First Thanksgiving Day.
a. Little George Washington.

BOOK OF LEGENDS—Horace E. Scudder.

B3 Grade

a. St. George and the Dragon.

FOUR OLD GREEKS—Jennie Hall.

B3 Grade

a. Greece and the Greeks.
a. Achilles.
a. Herakles.
a. Merry Dionysos.
a. How Alkestis Was Saved.

GRADED CLASSICS—First Reader.

B2 Grade

c, d. The Touch of Gold.
c, d. The Three Pigs.
c, d. The Lion and the Mouse.
c, d. The Three Bears - - Also in Vol. IV., Action, Imitation, and Fun Series.
c. The Old Woman and Her Pig.

GRADED CLASSICS—Second Reader.

A2 Grade

c.   Tom Thumb.
c.   Henny Penny.
c, d. The Town Mouse and the Country Mouse.
c, d. The Three Billy Goats.
c.   Jack and the Bean Stalk.

B3 Grade

c.   Hans and His Money.
c.   The Twelve Months.
c.   The Wise Men of Gotham.
c.   The Bell of Justice.
c.   Sweet and Low.
c.   Phaethon Drives the Sun Chariot.

HEART OF OAK BOOKS—FIRST BOOK (Nursery Rhymes and Jingles)

A2 Grade

c.   (First half of book.)

B3 Grade

c.   (Second half of book.)

HEART OF OAK BOOKS—SECOND BOOK.

A2 and B3 Grades

c, d. The Little Red Hen.
c, d. The Field Mouse and the Town Mouse.
c, d. The Mice, the Cat, and the Bell.
c, d. The Mouse and the Lion.
c, d. The Fox and the Grapes.
c, d. The Hare and the Tortoise.
c, d. The Fox and the Crow.
c, d. The Lark and Her Young.
c, d. Diamonds and Toads.
c, d. Cinderella.
c, d. The Sleeping Beauty.
c.   The Owl and the Pussy Cat.

SUNBONNET BABIES—E. O. Grover.

Second Grade

d.   Going to School.
d.   The Picnic.
d.   The Circus.

STORIES FOR CHILDREN—Mrs. Charles Lane.

B2 Grade

d.   The Crow and Her Children.
d.   Snow White and Rose Red.
d.   The Sleeping Beauty.

*ART LITERATURE READERS—BOOK I.

Second Grade

c, d.   Little Red Riding Hood.
c, d.   The Little Red Hen.
c.   The Three Ships.
c.   (Other poetic selections.)

*ART LITERATURE READERS—BOOK II.

Third Grade

c.   (Selections from and about Robert Louis Stevenson, Henry W. Longfellow, Sir Joshua Reynolds, etc.)

*ART LITERATURE READERS—BOOK III.

Third Grade

c.   (Selections from and about Eugene Field, Louise Alcott, Sir Edwin Landseer, Hans C. Andersen, Celia Thaxter, Thomas Gainsborough, Lewis Carroll and John G. Whittier.)

ACTION, IMITATION, AND FUN SERIES—Mara Pratt-Chadwick.

Second Grade

c, d.   The Three Pigs - - In Volume III.
c, d.   Three Little Kittens - - In Volume V.

---

*The whole Series, from Primer up, beautifully edited and illustrated.

c, d. Chicken Little - - In Volume V.
c, d. Red Riding Hood - - In Volume VI.
c, d. The Seven Kids - - In Volume VI.
c, d. Jack, the Giant Killer - - In Unnumbered Volume.

B3 Grade

c, d. Jack and the Bean Stalk - - In Unnumbered Volume.
c, d. Diamonds and Toads - - With above.
c, d. The Sleeping Beauty - - With above.
c, d. Hop o' My Thumb - - In Unnumbered Volume.
c, d. Tom Thumb - - With above.

BOOK OF PLAYS FOR LITTLE ACTORS—Johnston and Barnum.

Second and B3 Grades

(Excellent for dramatic Readings)

POETRY

N. B.—To be READ TO Children

THE POSY RING—Kate Douglas Wiggin and Nora A. Smith

NOTE.—This collection, as a whole, is excellent material for reading to children in primary grades.

SONGS OF THE TREE TOP AND MEADOW—Lida McMurry and Agnes Cook

(See Suggestions pp. 171-192)

A CHILD'S GARDEN OF VERSES—Robert Louis Stevenson

(All of these verses are excellent.)

LOVE SONGS OF CHILDHOOD—Eugene Field

The Rock-a-By Lady.
So, So, Rock-a-By, So!

The Night Wind.
The Duel.
The Shut-Eye Train.
Seein' Things.

RHYMES OF CHILDHOOD—James Whitcomb Riley

The Fishing Party.
The Runaway Boy.
The Raggedy Man.
Our Hired Man.
Granny's Come to Our House.
Little Orphant Annie.
A Boy's Mother.
The Boy Lives on Our Farm.
The Nine Little Goblins.
Out to Old Aunt Mary's.

POEMS—Henry W. Longfellow
Hiawatha (selections).
The Village Blacksmith.
The Children's Hour.
The Clock on the Stair.

POETRY
N. B.—To be MEMORIZED
Second and B Third Grades

A CHILD'S GARDEN OF VERSES—Robert Louis Stevenson

Bed in Summer.
The Swing.
My Shadow.
The Wind.
Rain.
Whole Duty of Children.
Time to Rise.
Happy Thought.

HEATH'S SECOND READER

GRADED CLASSICS—SECOND READER

OTHER POETRY

The Rainbow - - Wordsworth.
The Sweet Peas - - Keats.
He Prayeth Best - - Coleridge, Ancient Mariner.
The Year's at the Spring - - Browning, Pippa Passes.
The Seed - - In McMurry and Cook's Songs of the Tree
Top and Meadow.

NOTE.—See Three Years with the Poets, by Bertha Hazard, for good
selections for memorizing.

A-Third and Fourth Grades

CLARA M. PRESTON, Training Teacher

PROSE
A3 Grade

a, b. The Horse and the Olive - - Baldwin, Old Greek Stories.

a, b. William Tell in Ten Great Events - - Johonnet, Golden Rod Series.

a, b. Pandora - - Hawthorne, The Wonder Book.

a. Stories from the Bible - - Bible Stories for Young People.

a, b. Hercules and the Golden Apples - - Hawthorne, The Wonder Book.

c. Stories of Mother Goose Village - - Madge Bigham.

c. Robinson Crusoe - - McMurry, editor.

c. Selections from Art Literature Readers - - Books II. and III., Frances E. Chutter.

Thanksgiving Selections

a. Story of the First Thanksgiving - - Standish of Standish.

b. How the Vegetables Spent Thanksgiving - - Child Study Monthly, November, 1898.

b. The Squirrel's Thanksgiving - - Child Garden, November, 1898.

a. Story of the Pilgrims.

Christmas Selections

a, b. Christmas in Russia and England - - Plan Book.

a, b. Legends of the Christmas Time - - Plan Book.

b. Christmas in the Barn - - Wiggin, Story Hour.

b. Old Christmas - - Mary Howitt.

b. Why the Chimes Ring - - Kindergarten Plan Book.

b. The Legend of St. Christopher - - In 15, 16.

POETRY

A3 Grade

e. The Mountain and the Squirrel - - Emerson, in 2, 3, 4, 5, 21, 22, 23, 8, 24, 25, 26, 27, 1.

b. Baucis and Philemon - - Jonathan Swift, in 2, 28, 29, 23, 10, 2, 30.

e. Lost—Three Little Robins - - Mrs. C. F. Berry, in 4, 31.

b. A Bird's Nest - - Florence Perry, in 9.

b, e. Little Brown Hands - - M. H. Krout, in 1, 2, 32, 33, 34, 8, 35, 36.

b. The Fox and the Crow - - Jane Taylor, in 2.

b. The City Mouse and the Country Mouse - - Christina G. Rossetti, in 10.

b. Mrs. Speckled Feather's Family - - S. E. Eastman, in 4.

b. A Visit from St. Nicholas - - Clement Moore, in 3, 7, 37, 19, 40, 17, 38, 39, 2, 20, 1.

b, e. Wynken, Blynken, and Nod - - Eugene Field, in 8, 37, 41, 42, 20, 43.

b. The Fairy Folk - - John Keats, in 2.

b. Meadow Talk - - Caroline Leslie, in 8.

e. Drive the Nail Aright - - (Unknown), in 19.

e. "I Once Had a Sweet Little Doll" - - Chas. Kingsley, in 2.

e. Don't Give Up - - Phoebe Cary, in 18.

e. What the Winds Bring - - Stedman, in 17.

e. The Wonderful World - - Browne, in 8.

c, b. Selections from Art Literature Readers, Books II. and III. - - Frances E. Chutter.

HOME READING

A3 Grade

The True Story of George Washington - - E. S. Brook.

When Life is Young - - M. M. Dodge.

Stories of Great Americans for Little Americans - - Eggleston.

Letters from a Cat - - H. M. F. Jackson.

The Sleeping Beauty in the Wood - - A. Lang.

The Rambillicus Book - - McDougall.
Miss Muffet's Christmas Party - - Samuel Crothers.
Mother Goose Village - - Madge Bigham.
Eskimo Stories - - Mary E. Smith.
Moni, the Goat Boy - - Kunz.
Art Literature Readers, Books II. and III. - - Frances E.
    Chutter.

PROSE

Fourth Grade

c.   The Bee and the Gazelle - - Baldwin, Old Stories
       of the East.
c.   The Great Chief - - Baldwin, Old Stories of the
       East.
c.   The Garden of Delight - - Baldwin, Old Stories of
       the East.
c.   The Story of Joseph - - Baldwin, Old Stories of
       the East.
c.   The Two Brothers - - Baldwin, Old Stories of the
       East.
c.   The Flood of Waters - - Baldwin, Old Stories of
       the East.
b, c. Waste Not, Want Not - - Maria Edgeworth, *et
       al.*, in 12.
b, c. Order and Disorder - - Maria Edgeworth, *et al.*,
       in 12.
b, c. The Discontented Pendulum - - Maria Edgeworth,
       et al., in 12.
c.   Robinson Crusoe - - Defoe, Standard Lit. Series.
c.   Tales of Mother Goose - - M. V. O'Shea, Editor.
c.   Hans Andersen Stories - - Riverside Lit. Series.
c.   The New Year's Bargain - - Susan Coolidge.
c, d. Mischief's Thanksgiving - - Susan Coolidge.
b, c. The Wonderful Chair - - M. V. O'Shea.
b, c. The Water Babies - - Kingsley, in 13.
b, c. How Cedric Became a Knight - - Eliz. Harrison,
       in 13.
b, c. In the Reign of Coyote - - Catherine Chandler.
b, c. The Pony Engine - - Howells, Story Book.
b, c. Alice's Adventures in Wonderland - - Lewis Car-
       roll.

c.   Old Greek Stories - - Baldwin.

c.   (Selections from) Stepping Stones to Literature - - For Fourth Grades.

c.   Legend of the Gentian - - Mary S. Brooks, in 14.

c, d.   Two Little Confederates - - ‚Thos. N. Page.

POETRY

Fourth Grade

b.   The Fairies of the Caldon-Low - - Mary Howitt, in 2, 3, 1.

e.   Hurt No Living Thing - - Christina Rosetti, in 1.

b.   How the Leaves Came Down - - Susan Coolidge, in 1.

b, c.   The Spider and the Fly - - Mary Howitt, in 1, 2.

c.   The Way for Billy and Me - - James Hogg, in 1, 2.

c, e.   A Night with a Wolf - - Bayard Taylor, in 1.

c, e.   The Crow's Children - - Phoebe Cary, in 1.

b, c.   The Afternoon Nap - - Chas. Eastman, in 1.

b.   A Masquerade - - (Unknown), in 1.

b, c.   Jack Frost - - Hannah Gould, in 1.

b, c.   Jack in the Pulpit - - Clara Smith, in 1, 14, 48.

b, c, e.   The Sorrowful Sea Gull - - From Child World, in 1.

e.   The Sandpiper and I - - Celia Thaxter, in 1, 2, 4.

e.   The Tree - - Björnson, in 1.

c.   Good Night and Good Morning - - Lord Houghton, in 1, 2.

b.   The Bluebird - - Emily Miller, in 1.

b, c, e.   The Ant and the Cricket - - (Anonymous), in 2.

b.   Little Dandelion - - Helen Bostwick, in 1, 3, 20.

b.   Darius Green and His Flying Machine - - J. T. Trowbridge, Speaker's Garland, Vol. I.

e.   The Children's Hour - - Longfellow, Poems.

b.   John Gilpin - - W. L. Shepperd, in 3.

b.   The Vagabonds - - J. T. Trowbridge, in 4.

e.   The Nightingale and the Glow Worm - - Wm. Cowper, in 2, 5, 25, 17, 23, 20.

b.   The Kitten and the Falling Leaves - - Wm. Wordsworth, in 2, 5, 44, 28, 23, 20, 27.

b. The Leak in the Dike - - Phoebe Cary, in 18.
e. The Village Blacksmith - - H. W. Longfellow, in 5, 17, 44, 28, 8, 46, 40.
b, c. The Lamplighter - - R. L. Stevenson, in 5.
b. Seein' Things - - Eugene Field, in 6, 47, 41.
b. Picnic Time - - Eugene Field, in 6.

Thanksgiving Selections

b, c. The Pumpkin Glory - - Howells, Story Book.
c, d. Mischief's Thanksgiving - - Susan Coolidge.
c. "Chusey" (the November Story) - - Susan Coolidge, New Year's Bargain.
b. Thanksgiving Day - - Lydia Child, in 1.

Christmas Selections

b, c. How the Cat Kept Christmas (the December Story) - - Susan Coolidge, New Year's Bargain.
b. Adaptation from Ben Hur - - Lew Wallace.
b, c. Babouscha, Santa, and Family - - Child Garden, December, 1893.
b, c. The Strange Child's Christmas - - (From the German), in 3.
b, c. A Visit to the Baby King - - Child Garden, December, 1899.
b, c. Christmas Every Day - - Howells, Story Book.

SOURCES

1. Child Life - - Edited by Whittier.
2. Open Sesame - - Vol. I.
3. Poetry for Children - - S. Eliot.
4. Voices for the Speechless - - A. Firth.
5. The Listening Child - - Thatcher.
6. Love Songs of Childhood - - E. Field.
7. A Child's Book of Poetry - - Edna Turpin.
8. Graded Memory Selection - - Waterman, et al.
9. Stepping Stones to Literature - - For Third Grades.
10. Golden Numbers - - Wiggin and Smith.
11. Old Stories of the East - - Baldwin.
12. Waste Not, Want Not - - Maria Edgeworth, et al.
13. Stepping Stones to Literature - - For Fourth Grades.

14. Language Readers - - Third Reader, Baker and Carpenter.
15. Language Readers - - Fourth Reader, Baker and Carpenter.
16. Stories of the Saints - - Chenoweth.
17. New Library of Poetry and Song - - Bryant.
18. Alice and Phoebe Cary's Poems.
19. Selections for Memorizing - - Foster and Williams.
20. The Posy Ring - - Wiggin and Smith.
21. Arbor Day Manual - - C. B. Skinner.
22. Book of Verse for Children - - E. V. Lucas.
23. Children's Garland from the Best Poets - - C. Patmore.
24. Poetry for Home and School - - A. C. Brackett and I. M. Eliot.
25. Poetry of the Seasons - - M. I. Lovejoy, Compiler.
26. Progressive Speaker - - National Pub. Co.
27. Pieces to Speak - - H. H. Ballard.
28. Fireside Encyclopedia of Poetry - - H. T. Coates.
29. Humorous Poetry of the English Language - - J. Parton.
30. Reading and Recitation, No. 11 - - Werner.
31. Lincoln Literary Collection - - J. P. McCaskey.
32. Choice Pieces for Little People - - T. S. Dennison.
33. Choice Selections, One Hundred, No. 12 - - Penn Pub. Co.
34. The Favorite Speaker - - La Moille and Parsons.
35. School Reader, Vol. 2 - - Harper.
36. Tommy's First Speaker - - Donohue & Co.
37. American Anthology - - E. C. Stedman.
38. Every Day in the Year - - James and Mary Ford.
39. The Household Book of Poetry - - Charles Dana.
40. Choice Literature, Intermediate, Book I. - - S. Williams.
41. Eugene Field Book - - Burt and Cable.
42. Hand Book of Best Reading - - S. H. Clark.
43. With Trumpet and Drum - - Eugene Field.
44. Best Short Poems of Nineteenth Century - - W. S. Lord.
45. Best Selections, No. 7 - - Penn Pub. Co.

46. Prize Poetical Speaker - - H. A. Dickerman & Son.
47. Best Selections, No. 24 - - Penn Pub. Co.
48. Nature in Verse for Children - - Lovejoy.

HOME READING

Fourth Grade

Fifty Famous Stories Retold - - Baldwin.
The Birds' Christmas Carol - - Kate D. Wiggin.
The Call of the Wild - - Jack London.
Two Little Confederates - - Thos. N. Page.
New Year's Bargain - - Susan Coolidge.
Queer Little People - - H. B. Stowe.
The Wonder Book - - N. Hawthorne.
Robinson Crusoe - - D. Defoe.
Little Pepper Series - - M. Sidney.
Little Colonel Series - - Johnston.
Tales from Shakespeare - - Lamb.
Uncle Remus - - J. C. Harris.
Swiss Family Robinson - - Wyss.
Beautiful Joe - - M. Saunders.
Hans Brinker or the Silver Skates - - M. M. Dodge.
Story of a Brownie - - Maria Mulock.
Wizard of Oz - - Baum.
Docas, the Indian Boy - - Mrs. D. Snedden.
Little Lord Fauntleroy - - F. H. Burnett.
Sara Crewe - - F. H. Burnett.
Little Saint Elizabeth - - F. H. Burnett.
Editha's Burglar - - F. H. Burnett.
Mischief's Thanksgiving - - S. Coolidge.
The Little Lame Prince - - M. Mulock.
The Prince and the Pauper - - S. Clemens.
The Jungle Book - - Kipling.
Jack Book Series - - George B. Grinnell.
Zitkala-Sa, Old Indian Legends - - Pub. by Ginn & Co.
Little Lucy's Wonderful Globe - - Charlotte Young.
The Red True Story Book - - Andrew Lang.
The Rambillicus Book - - McDougall.
The Boy Settlers - - Brooks.
A Boy on a Farm - - Abbott.
Ways of Wood Folk - - Long.

Wilderness Ways - - Long.
Captain January - - L. E. Richards.
Ernest Thompson Seton's Books.
Lolami, The Little Cliff Dweller - - Clara Bayliss.
Viking Tales - - Jennie Hall.
Art Literature Readers, Books II. and III. - - Frances E.
  Chutter.

Fifth Grade

KATE F. OSGOOD, Training Teacher

b, c.	The Story of the Rhinegold - - Anna Alice Chapin.
b, c.	The Norse Stories - - Hamilton Wright Mabie.
b.	Bible Stories - - Moulton.
b, c.	Old Stories of the East - - James Baldwin.
b.	Stories of the Bible - - Ed. Publishing Co.
c, d.	King of the Golden River - - John Ruskin.
c, e.	The Bell of Atri - - H. W. Longfellow.
c, e.	The Emperor's Bird's Nest - - H. W. Longfellow.
c, e.	The Arrow and the Song - - H. W. Longfellow.
c, e.	Hiawatha's Childhood - - H. W. Longfellow.
c, e.	Hiawatha's Hunting - - H. W. Longfellow.
c, e.	Hiawatha's Friends - - H. W. Longfellow.
c, e.	An Order for a Picture - - Alice Cary.
c, e.	The Barefoot Boy - - J. G. Whittier.
c, e.	Robert of Lincoln - - W. C. Bryant.
b, c.	The O'Lincoln Family - - Flagg.
b, c.	The Bob-o-Link in Birds of Spring - - Washington Irving, Wolfert's Roost.
b, c, e.	The Bloodless Sportsman - - S. W. Foss.
b, c, d.	The Pied Piper of Hamelin - - Robert Browning.
c, e.	The Apple Blossoms - - Wm. Wesley Martin.
c, e.	*Columbus - - Joaquin Miller.
c, e.	*The Landing of the Pilgrims - - Mrs. Hemans.
c, e.	The Voice of Spring - - Mrs. Hemans.
c, d, a, b.	Merry Adventures of Robin Hood - - Howard Pyle.
c.	The Wonder Clock - - Howard Pyle.
c, e.	The American Flag - - Drake.

*To be taken in connection with History.

c, e.	The Brook - - Tennyson.
c, e.	The First Bluebird - - Jas. Whitcomb Riley.
c, e.	Rain in Summer - - Longfellow.
c, e.	Before the Rain - - T. B. Aldrich.
c, e.	After the Rain - - T. B. Aldrich.

Morning Exercises

b.	Mowgli's Brothers - - Kipling, Jungle Book.
b.	Kaa's Hunting - - Kipling, Jungle Book.
b.	Rikki-Tikki-Tavi - - Kipling, Jungle Book.
b.	The White Seal - - Kipling, Jungle Book.
b.	*Grandfather's Chair - - Hawthorne.
b.	†The Pastoral Bee and The Idyl of the Honey Bee - - John Burroughs, Birds and Bees.
b.	†Pepacton - - John Burroughs.
b.	†Sharp Eyes - - John Burroughs.
b.	†Squirrels and Other Fur Bearers - - John Burroughs.
b.	†True Bird Stories - - Olive Thorne Miller.
b.	†The Story of a Salmon - - David Starr Jordan.
b, c.	Heidi - - Johanna Spyri.
b.	A Boy's Town - - W. D. Howells.
b.	Brave Little Holland - - Wm. E. Griffis.

HOME READING

Fifth Grade

Matka and Kotik - - David Starr Jordan.
The Jungle Book - - Rudyard Kipling.
The Second Jungle Book - - Rudyard Kipling.
Wild Animals I Have Known - - E. Thompson Seton.
Trail of the Sandhill Stag - - E. Thompson Seton.
Story of a Bad Boy - - T. B. Aldrich.
Being a Boy - - C. D. Warner.
Cudjo's Cave - - Trowbridge.
Robinson Crusoe - - Defoe.
Swiss Family Robinson - - Wyss.
Boy Emigrants - - N. Brooks.
Hans Brinker or The Silver Skates - - M. M. Dodge.

---

*To be taken in connection with History.
†To be taken in connection with Nature Study.

Land of Pluck - - M. M. Dodge.
*Old Times in the Colonies - - C. C. Coffin.
*Home Life in Colonial Days - - Alice Morse Earle.
*Child Life in Colonial Days - - Alice Morse Earle.
Family Flights - - E. E. Hale and Susan Hale.
Book of Golden Deeds - - Charlotte M. Yonge.
Stories of the Golden Age - - James Baldwin.
Story of Siegfried - - James Baldwin.
*Little Daughters of the Revolution - - Nora Perry.
Boyhood in Norway - - H. H. Boyesen.
Modern Vikings - - H. H. Boyesen.
Magellan - - George M. Towle.

*To be taken in connection with History.

Sixth Grade

SARAH E. WOODBURY, Training Teacher

POETRY
B6 Grade

b, c.	Sir Patrick Spens - - In 5, 12.
b, c.	Birds of Killingworth - - Longfellow, in 5, 13.
b, c, d, e.	Paul Revere's Ride - - Longfellow, in 13.
b, c, e.	Concord Hymn - - Emerson, in 5, 12.
b, c.	How They Brought the Good News from Ghent to Aix - - Browning, in 9, 4, 5, 11.
b, c, e.	Breathes There a Man? - - Scott, Lay of the Last Minstrel.
b, c, e.	Soldier, Rest - - Scott, Lady of the Lake.
b, c, e.	Song of the Chattahoochee - - Lanier, in 3.
b, c.	The Walrus and the Carpenter - - L. Carroll, Alice in Wonderland.
b, c, e.	The Blue and the Gray - - Finch, in 12.
b, c, e.	The Destruction of Sennacherib - - Byron, in 7.
b, c, d, e.	Horatius at the Bridge - - Macaulay, in 2, 11, 4.
b, c.	Rienzi's Address to the Romans - - Mitford, in 11.
b, c, e.	Battle Hymn of the Republic - - Julia Ward Howe, in 11, 12.

PROSE
B6 Grade

a, b, c, d.	Christmas Carol - - Dickens, in 13.
b, c, d.	Tanglewood Tales - - Hawthorne, in 13.
a, b, c, d.	Greek Heroes - - Kingsley, in 13.
a, b, c.	Adventures of Ulysses - - In 2.
a, b, c.	Rome and the Romans - - In 2.
a, b, c.	The Beginning of Rome - - In 2.
a, b, c.	The Man without a Country - - Hale, in 13.

b, c.   The Dying Gladiator - - Byron, in 13.
b, c, d.   Old Pipes and the Dryad - - Stockton, Fanciful
           Tales.
b, c, d.   Bee Man of Orne - - Stockton, Fanciful Tales.
b, c, d.   Clocks of Rondaine - - Stockton, Fanciful Tales.
b.   The Odyssey - - Palmer, in 13.
c.   Most of the prose selections in Heath's Fifth Reader.

POETRY
A6 Grade

b, c, e.   Ye Mariners of England - - T. Campbell, in 7,
           9, 10, 12.
b, c, e.   Abou Ben Adhem - - L. Hunt, in 5, 9.
b, c.   Allin a Dale - - In 1, 5, 12.
b, c, e.   The Cloud - - Shelley, in 1, 8, 10.
b, c, e.   The Daffodils - - Wordsworth, in 1, 4, 6, 8, 10.
b, c, e.   Bugle Call - - Tennyson, in 1, 6, 9, 10.
b, c, e.   Hark, Hark the Lark . - - Shakespeare, in 1, 6.
b, c, e.   Over Hill and Dale - - Shakespeare, in 1, 8.
b, c, e.   When Icicles Hang - - Shakespeare, in 1, 8.
b, c, e.   Orpheus and His Lute - - Shakespeare, in 1, 6.
b, c, d, e. Rising of 1776 - - Read, in 1.
b, c, e.   Selections from Hiawatha - - Longfellow, in 1,
           13.
b, c, e.   Planting of the Apple Tree - - Bryant, in 1, 13.
b, c, e.   Burial of Sir John Moore - - Wolfe, in 1, 10, 11,
           12.
b, c, e.   The Ivy Green - - Dickens, in 1, 8.
b, c, e.   The Arrow and the Song - - Longfellow, in 1,
           13.
b, c, e.   The Day is Done - - Longfellow, in 1, 13.
b, c, e.   The Lady of Shalott - - Tennyson, in 13.
b, c.   The Inchcape Rock - - Southey, in 10.

PROSE
A6 Grade

a, b, c, d. Merry Adventures of Robin Hood - - Pyle.
a, b, c, d. Story of King Arthur and His Knights - - Pyle.
b, c.   Story of Roger - - Andrews, Ten Boys.
a, b, c.   Red Cap Tales - - Crockett.

SOURCES

1. Heath Reader - - Book V.
2. Stepping Stones to Literature - - For Sixth Grades.
3. Stepping Stones to Literature - - For Seventh Grades.
4. Lights to Literature - - Book IV.
5. Heart of Oak Books - - Fourth Book.
6. Heart of Oak Books - - Fifth Book.
7. Heart of Oak Books - - Sixth Book.
8. Poetry of the Seasons - - Compiled by Mary I. Love-joy.
9. Book of Famous Poems - - Compiled by T. B. Aldrich.
10. The Listening Child - - Compiled by Lucy Thacher.
11. Open Sesame - - Vol. II.
12. Poetry of the People - - Compiled by Charles Mills Gayley and M. C. Flaherty.
13. Author's Work.

HOME READING

Sixth Grade

Story of a Bad Boy - - T. B. Aldrich.
Juan and Juanita - - F. C. Baylor.
Rab and His Friends - - J. Brown.
Heroes of the Middle West - - M. H. Catherwood.
Boots and Saddles - - Mrs. E. Custer.
Two Years Before the Mast - - R. H. Dana.
Stories for Boys - - R. H. Dana.
Matka and Kotik - - David Starr Jordan.
The Jungle Book - - Rudyard Kipling.
The Second Jungle Book - - Rudyard Kipling.
Crusoe's Island - - F. A. Oher.
Trail of the Sandhill Stag - - E. Thompson Seton.
Magellan - - G. M. Towle.
Drake, the Sea King of Devon - - G. M. Towle.
Vasco de Gama - - G. M. Towle.
Heroes and Martyrs of Invention - - G. M. Towle.
Swiss Family Robinson - - J. D. Wyss.
The Daisy Chain - - Charlotte Yonge.
Pillars of the House - - Charlotte Yonge.

Boy Hunters - - T. B. Reed.
Indian Boyhood - - Chas. Eastman.
Famous Men of Greece - - Haaren and Poland.
Famous Men of Rome - - Haaren and Poland.
Famous Men of the Middle Ages - - Haaren and Poland.
The Boy Captive of Old Deerfield - - M. P. W. Smith.
Ways of Wood Folks - - Wm. J. Long.
Wilderness Ways - - Wm. J. Long.
Secrets of the Woods - - Wm. J. Long.
The Story of Dago - - Annie F. Johnston.
The Biography of a Grizzly - - Ernest Thompson Seton.
Two Little Savages - - Ernest Thompson Seton.
Lives of the Hunted - - Ernest Thompson Seton.
The Cricket on the Hearth - - C. Dickens.
Dombey and Son - - C. Dickens.
Hans Brinker or The Silver Skates - - M. M. Dodge.
A Boy's Town - - W. D. Howells.
The Flight of Pony Baker - - W. D. Howells.
Silver Medal Stories - - J. T. Trowbridge.
Boyhood in Norway - - H. H. Boyesen.
Little Men - - Louise M. Alcott.
Little Women - - Louise M. Alcott.
Jo's Boys - - Louise M. Alcott.
Cadet Days - - Chas. King.
Camp Mates - - Kirk Monroe.
Canoe Mates - - Kirk Monroe.
Snow-shoes and Sledges - - Kirk Monroe.
Two Little Knights of Kentucky - - A. F. Johnston.

Seventh Grade

M. BELLE STEVER, Training Teacher

PROSE
B7 Grade

c, d.	Rip Van Winkle - - Irving, in 5.
b and c.	Rab and His Friends - - J. Brown, in 10.
c.	The Man without a Country - - Hale, in 11.
b and c, d.	Little Nell - - Dickens, in 7, 9.
b and c, d.	Little David - - Dickens, in 7, 9.
c.	Wee Willie Winkie - - Kipling, in 11.
b and c.	Treasure Island - - Stevenson, in 8.

POETRY
B7 Grade

c.	Grandmother's Story of Bunker Hill - - Holmes, in 11.
b and c.	Courtship of Miles Standish - - Longfellow, in 2, 7, 9.
b and c.	Prisoner of Chillon - - Byron, in 1, 7.
c.	Little People of the Snow - - Bryant, in 11.
c.	Sella - - Bryant, in 11.
c.	Horatius at the Bridge - - Macaulay, in 1.
c.	Incident of the French Camp - - Browning, in 4.
c.	Lochinvar - - Scott, in 1, 6.
c.	Lochiel's Warning - - Campbell, in 1.
e, c.	Concord Hymn - - Emerson, in 11.
e, c.	The Bugle Song - - Tennyson, in 5, 13.
e, c.	To a Waterfowl - - Bryant, in 11.
e, c.	Flower in the Crannied Wall - - Tennyson, in 12.
e, c.	The Eagle - - Tennyson, in 12.

e, c.   To a Dandelion - - Lowell, in 5.
e, c.   The Cloud - - Shelley, in 6.
c.   Brooks' Reader - - VI., VII., and VIII. com-
          bined.

PROSE

A7 Grade

c.   The Great Stone Facé - - Hawthorne, in 9.
c.   Snow Image - - Hawthorne, in 7, 9.
b and c.   The Gold Bug - - Poe, in 8.
b and c, d.   Legend of Sleepy Hollow - - Irving, in 2.
c.   Legend of the Moor's Legacy - - Irving, in 2.
d, c.   The Pot of Broth - - Yeats, in 11.
b and c.   Girls Who Became Famous - - Sara K. Bol-
              ton, in 11.
c.   The Heights of Abraham - - Parkman, in 2.
c.   The Discovery of Lake Champlain - - Park-
              man, in 2.
b and c, d.   The Spy - - Cooper, in 7.

POETRY

A7 Grade

b and c, e.   Evangeline - - Longfellow, in 9.
b, c and e.   The Building of the Ship - - Longfellow, in 2.
c.   King Robert of Sicily - - Longfellow, in 11.
b, c, e.   Snow-bound - - Whittier, in 9.
b, c, e.   Rhyme of the Ancient Mariner - - Coleridge,
              in 5.
c.   The Ballad of East and West - - Kipling, in 4.
c.   The Revenge - - Tennyson, in 5.
c.   Hervé Riel - - Browning, in 3, 5.
c.   Marco Bozzaris - - Fitz-Green Halleck, in 2.
e, c.   Daffodils - - Wordsworth, in 5.
e, c.   To a Cuckoo - - Wordsworth, in 6.
e, c.   To a Skylark - - Shelley, in 6.
e.   The Laughing Chorus - - In 15.

SOURCES

1. Stepping Stones to Literature - - For Sixth Grades.
2. Stepping Stones to Literature - - For Seventh Grades.

3. Stepping Stones to Literature - - For Higher Grades.
4. Heart of Oak Books - - Fourth Book.
5. Heart of Oak Books - - Fifth Book.
6. Heart of Oak Books - - Sixth Book.
7. University Standard Literature Series.
8. Canterbury Classics Series.
9. Riverside Classics Series.
10. Modern Classics.
11. Author's Work.
12. Open Sesame, Vol. I.
13. Open Sesame, Vol. II.
14. Open Sesame, Vol. III.
15. Emerson's Evolution of Expression, Vol. I.

HOME READING

Seventh Grade

Winning His Way - - C. C. Coffin.
Boots and Saddles - - Mrs. E. Custer.
By Right of Conquest - - Henty.
Flamingo Feather - - Munro.
Westward Ho - - Kingsley.
A Nameless Nobleman - - Austin.
Peasant and Prince - - Martineau.
Last of the Mohicans - - Cooper.
Fair God - - Wallace.
A Tale of Two Cities - - Dickens.
Book of Golden Deeds - - Yonge.
House of Seven Gables - - Hawthorne.
Alice of Old Vincennes - - Thompson.
Richard Carvel - - Churchill.
Hugh Wynne - - Mitchell.
Midshipman Paulding - - Seawell.
The Hoosier Schoolboy - - Eggleston.
At the Back of the North Wind - - McDonald.
Red Cap Tales - - Crockett.
Pilgrim's Progress - - Bunyan.
The Story of My Life - - Helen Keller.
Life of Washington - - E. E. Hale.
The American Boy's Handy Book - - Dan C. Beard.

The American Girl's Handy Book - - Lina and Adelia
  Beard.
Wild Animals I Have Known - - E. Thompson Seton.
How to Know the Butterflies - - Comstock.
The First Book of Birds - - Olive Thorne Miller.
Historic Girls - - E. S. Brooks.

Eighth Grade

ELIZABETH T. SULLIVAN, Training Teacher

PROSE

c.   Ninety-three - - Hugo, in 14.

b, c.   A Perfect Tribute (to Lincoln) - - Andrews, in 23.

b.   The Other Wise Man - - Van Dyke, in 1.

c.   Silas Marner - - Eliot, in 1.

b, c.   The Heart of Old Hickory - - Dromgoole, in 1.

b, c.   The Lost Necklace - - Maupassant, in 22.

c.   Lorna Doone - - Blackmore, in 1.

a, b, c. The Stories of Sir Galahad - - In 9, 18, 19.

a, b, c. The Stories of Lohengrin - - In 20.

a, b, c. The Stories of Parsifal - - In 24.

POETRY

Longer Poems

c.   The Vision of Sir Launfal - - Lowell, in 1, 11.

b, d.   Selections from the Idylls of the King - - Tennyson, in 1, 2, 4, 9.

c.   Sohrab and Rustum - - Arnold, in 1, 15.

b.   The Legend of Bregenz - - Proctor, in 1.

b, c.   The Lady of the Lake - - Scott, in 1.

c.   Snow-bound - - Whittier, in 1, 11.

c.   Seven Seas - - Kipling, in 1.

c.   The Ancient Mariner - - Coleridge, in 1.

b.   Thanatopsis - - Bryant, in 1, 10.

SHORT POEMS OF THE DIFFERENT ENGLISH-SPEAKING PEOPLE
England

b.   Recessional - - Kipling, in 21.

e.   Crossing the Bar - - Tennyson, in 1, 9.

e. To a Skylark - - Shelley, in 1, 7, 10.
e. To a Skylark - - Wordsworth, in 1, 7, 10.
e. The Daffodils - - Wordsworth, in 1, 8.
e. Self Dependence - - Arnold, in 1, 7.

Scotland

e. Flow Gently, Sweet Afton - - Burns, in 1.
e. Highland Mary - - Burns, in 1.
e. To a Mountain Daisy - - Burns, in 1.
e. To a Mouse - - Burns, in 1.
e. For a' That and a' That - - Burns, in 1, 2, 6, 9.

Ireland

e. The Meeting of the Waters - - Moore, in 1.
e. Erin, the Smile and the Tear in Thine Eye - - Moore, in 1.
e. O, Blame Not the Bard - - Moore, in 1.
e. Believe Me if All Those Endearing Young Charms - - Moore, in 1.

America

e. The Rhodora - - Emerson, in 1.
e. To a Waterfowl - - Bryant, in 1, 5.
e. The Chambered Nautilus - - Holmes, in 1.
e. Hymn to the Night - - Longfellow, in 1.

c, b. **Some Simple ESSAYS (selected parts):**

- - Emerson, in 1.
- - Bacon, in 1.

Some Simple ORATIONS (selected parts):

b. Reply to Hayne - - Webster, in 25, 26.
b. Second Inaugural Address - - Lincoln, in 2, 3, 10.
c, e. Gettysburg Address - - Lincoln, in 23, 3, 9, 2, 26.
b. On Conciliation with America - - Burke, in 13.
b. Farewell Address - - Washington, in 2, 3.
b. First Oration on Bunker Hill Monument - - Webster, in 3.

DRAMA

c, d.   The Merchant of Venice - - Shakespeare, in 12.
c, d.   Julius Cæsar - - Shakespeare, in 12.

NOTE.—The working course in literature for the Eighth Grade in the Training School consists of different interpretations of the "Quest of the Holy Grail," with intensive study of "The Vision of Sir Launfal," analysis and reading of "Silas Marner," and either "Julius Cæsar" or "The Merchant of Venice." Impersonation of character and dramatic reading are a part of the regular recitation. For the last few years scenes selected from the literature of the grade have furnished material for closing exercises.

SOURCES

1. Author's work.
2. Stepping Stones to Literature - - For Sixth Grades.
3. Stepping Stones to Literature - - For Seventh Grades.
4. Stepping Stones to Literature - - For Higher Grades.
5. Heart of Oak Books - - Fourth Book.
6. Heart of Oak Books - - Fifth Book.
7. Heart of Oak Books - - Sixth Book.
8. Heath's Fifth Reader.
9. Open Sesame, Vol. II.
10. Open Sesame, Vol. III.
11. Riverside Literature Series.
12. Hudson Edition of Shakespeare.
13. Burke - - Select Works, Vol. I., edited by Payne.
14. Standard Literature Series, abridged, University Pub. Co.
15. Eclectic English Classics.
16. Hamlin - - Pictures from English Literature.
17. C. H. Hanson - - Stories of the Days of King Arthur.
18. Frances M. Greene - - King Arthur and His Court.
19. Lanier - - Boys' King Arthur.
20. Chapin - - Wonder Tales from Wagner.
21. Kipling - - Recessional, illustrated by Harper and Tobin.
22. The Odd Number - - Maupassant.

23. Andrews - - The Perfect Tribute, Scribner's Sons; **also** in Scribner's Magazine (July, 1906), Vol. 40, pp. 17-24.
24. Ford - - Message of the Mystics.
25. Johnston-Woodburn - - American Eloquence, Section IV.
26. Johnston-Woodburn - - American Eloquence, Section VII.

HOME READING

Eighth Grade

Captains Courageous - - Kipling.
Treasure Island - - Stevenson.
Kidnapped - - Stevenson.
Two Years Before the Mast - - Dana.
The Last of the Mohicans - - Cooper.
.Ivanhoe - - Scott.
Kenilworth - - Scott.
The Last Days of Pompeii - - Lytton.
Ben Hur - - Wallace.
Fabiola - - Wiseman.
Calista - - Wiseman.
The Bleak House - - Dickens.
David Copperfield - - Dickens.
Tom Brown's School Days - - Hughes.
Tom Brown at Rugby - - Hughes.
Famous Types of Womanhood - - Bolton.
Men of Iron - - H. Pyle.
Stories from the Bible - - A. J. Church.
Uncle Tom's Cabin - - Stowe.
Tom Sawyer - - Mark Twain.
Vicar of Wakefield - - Goldsmith.
Les Miserables - - Hugo.
Don Quixote - - Cervantes.
John Halifax, Gentleman - - Murdock.
Arthur Bonnicastle - - J. G. Holland.
A Midsummer Night's Dream - - Shakespeare.
Heroes of Chivalry - - Dodd, Mead & Co., N. Y.
Boys' King Arthur - - Lanier.

Message of the Mystics - - Ford.
Life of Lincoln - - Hanks, American Mag., Feb., 1908.
He Knew Lincoln - - Tarbell.

General References

REFERENCES ON
PEDAGOGY OF LITERATURE

Fred A. Howe   Ella G. Wood

Adler, Felix: The Moral Education of Children.

Bates, Arlo: Talks on the Study of Literature.

Carpenter, Baker, and Scott: The Teaching of English.

Chubb, Percival: The Teaching of English.

Colby, J. Rose: Literature and Life in School.

Corson, Hiram: The Aims of Literary Study.

Dowden, Edward: New Studies in Literature.

Hudson, Henry N.: English in Schools, **Preface** to The Merchant of Venice, Ginn & Co.

MacClintock, Porter Lander: Literature in the Elementary School.

McMurry, Charles A.: Special Method in the Reading of Complete English Classics.

Trent, Wm. P.: The Authority of Criticism and Other Essays.

Warner, Charles D.: The Relation of Literature to Life.

REFERENCES ON
TELLING OF STORIES

Beatrice Chandler Patton   Everett Shepardson

Bryant, Sara Cone: How to Tell Stories to Children.

Bryant, Sara Cone: Some Suggestions for the Story-teller and Story-telling in Teaching English - - Stories to Tell to Children, pp. IX-XLVII.

Earhart, Lida B.: The Story in the Primary Grades - - Teachers College Record, Vol. 8, pp. 133-144.

Hassler, Harriot E.: Work with Children and Schools in the Portland (Oregon) Public Library - - Library Journal (April, 1905), Vol. 30, pp. 214-217.

MacClintock, Porter Lander: Literature in the Elementary School, *passim*.

Ware, Allison: The Teacher as Story-teller - - An Elementary Course of Study in Literature (San Francisco State Normal School Bulletin No. 5, New Series), pp. 21-23.

————: Story Telling to Children (accompanying story lists from Norse Mythology and the Nibelungenlied, 48 pp., price, $0.20) - - Carnegie Library of Pittsburgh (Bulletin), 1903.

————: Story Telling to Children - - Carnegie Library of Pittsburgh (Monthly Bulletin), Dec., 1905, pp. 271-273.

————: Brief Account of the Story Hour Conducted by the Children's Department (accompanying list of Good Stories to Tell to Children under Twelve Years of Age, 31 pp., price, $0.05) - - Carnegie Library of Pittsburgh (Bulletin), 1906.

REFERENCES ON
DRAMATIZATION

Beatrice Chandler Patton   Josephine E. Seaman
Sarah E. Woodbury   Everett Shepardson

Elementary School Teacher (including Vol. 1, Course of
Study)

Ashleman, Lorley A.: The Teaching of a Language in the
Elementary School - - Vol. 5, pp. 285-291.

Atwood, Harriet Bradley: in First Grade (Curriculum) - -
Course of Study, Vol. 1, pp. 157-158.

Bass, Willard Streeter: in Fifth Grade (Curriculum) - -
Course of Study, Vol. 1, pp. 165-168.

Blaine, Anita McCormick: The Dramatic in Education - -
Vol. 4, pp. 554-558. ·

Chubb, Percival: Function of the Festival in School Life
- - Vol. 4. pp. 559-565.

Colvin, Stephen S.: The Child's World of Imagination - -
Vol. 6, pp. 327-342.

Dryer, Mabel Elizabeth: The Making of a Play (Seventh
Grade) - - Vol. 8, pp. 423-436.

Fleming, Martha: The Making of a Play (Sixth Grade) - -
Vol. 8, pp. 15-23.

Fleming, Martha: Must it Be a Lost Art? - - Vol. 4, pp.
541-553.

Fleming, Martha: in Speech, Oral Reading, and Dramatic
Art - - Course of Study, Vol. 1, pp. 211-214, 873-879; ·
Vol. 2, pp. 59-63 (including Old Pipes and the Dryad—Sixth
Grade), 635-652 (including A Play of Galahad—Third
Grade).

Fleming, Martha: The Woodman and the Goblins (story by
John Duncan) - - Vol. 4, pp. 594-600.

Foster, Edith B.: in Sixth Grade (Curriculum) - - Course
of Study, Vol. 1, pp. 168-171.

Hall, Jennie: Lionel of Orkney—A One-act Play (Eighth
Grade) - - Vol. 5, pp. 29-35.

Hall, Jennie: Some Plans of Dramatic Representation in
Primary Grades - - Vol. 4, pp. 566-578.

Hollister, Antoinette: in Second Grade (Curriculum) - -
Course of Study, Vol. 1, pp. 159-160.

MacClintock, Porter Lander: Concerning Drama and Oratory in the School - - Vol. 4, pp. 601-604.

MacClintock, Porter Lander: Literature in the Elementary School - - Vol. 3, pp. 87-95.

Mitchell, Clara Isabel: in Fourth Grade (Curriculum) - - Course of Study, Vol. 1, pp. 163-165.

Norton, Edward L. and Ashleman, Lorley Ada: Dramatics in the Teaching of a Foreign Language - - Vol. 6, pp. 33-39.

Payne, Bertha: Dramatic Play in the Kindergarten - - Vol. 4, pp. 588-593.

Purcell, Helen Elizabeth: Children's Dramatic Interest and How This May Be Utilized in Education - - Vol. 7, pp. 510-518.

Sherz, Anna Talea: The Dramatic Sense, an Aid in Learning a Foreign Language - - Vol. 4, pp. 579-587.

Thorne-Thomson, Gudren: The Troll's Christmas - - Vol. 8, pp. 210-215.

Van Hoesen, Gertrude: in Third Grade (Curriculum) - - Course of Study, Vol. 1, pp. 160-162.

————: The Course of Study of the Elementary School in English - - Vol. 8, pp. 524-533, *passim*.

Teachers College Record

Barney, Mabel I.: The Dramatic Instinct in the Elementary School (including the Pilgrim Play—Sixth Grade) - - Vol. 8, pp. 118-126.

Barnum, Edith C.: in Literature - - Vol. 7, pp. 66 *et seq.* (Hiawatha—First Grade).

Batchelder, Mildred I.: in Reading and Literature - - Vol. 7, p. 398 (Alice in Wonderland—Third Grade).

Kirchway, Mary F.: in Literature - - Vol. 8, p. 172 (Robin Hood—Sixth Grade).

Peabody, Mary G.: in Literature and Reading - - Vol. 8, p. 58 (Minotaur—Fifth Grade).

Robbins, Ida E.: in Reading and Literature - - Vol. 8, p. 3 (Lady of the Lake—Fourth Grade).

Welles, Katherine: in Reading and Literature - - Vol. 7, p. 370 (Robinson Crusoe—Second Grade).

Books and Other Articles

Addams, Jane: Work and Play as Factors in Education - - The Chautauquan, Vol. 42, pp. 25 *et seq.*

Blaisdell: Potent Factors in Teaching Oral Reading and Oral Language Dramatizing - - Journal of Education (July, 1907), pp. 125 *et seq.*

Buckbee, Anna: Use of Dramatization in Teaching History - - New York Teachers' Monographs, Vol. 5 (March, 1903), pp. 106-117.

Chubb, Percival: Avenues of Language-Expression in the Elementary School - - N. E. A. Report, 1904, pp. 452-459.

Craig, Anne Throop: The Development of a Dramatic Element in Education ‑ - Pedagogical Seminary, Vol. 15, pp. 75-81.

Doyle, Rhoads: Teaching Hiawatha to a 3A class - - New York Teachers' Monographs, Vol. 7 (March, 1905), pp. 41-45.

Doyle, Rhoads: Reading the Pied Piper of Hamelin to a 4A class - - *do*, pp. 48-51.

Freytag, Gustav: Technique of the Drama, Chapters 1 and 2.

Keith, John A. H.: in Sub-Stages of Image Thinking - - Elementary Education, pp. 204-209.

MacClintock, Porter Lander: Drama - - Literature in the Elementary School, Chapter 13.

McGuire: The Dramatic Instinct as Related to Oral Reading - - New York Teachers' Monographs (June, 1902).

Nicholson, Anne M.: in Language in the Grades - - California Education (San José), Vol. 1 (Dec., 1905), pp. 14 and 15 (First Grade); 22 (Second Grade); 24, 26-28 (Third Grade).

O'Shea, M. V.: The Development of Inhibition - - Dynamic Factors in Education, Chapter 1.

————: The Dramatization of School Work - - The Outlook, Vol. 89 (May, 1908), pp. 93-94.

————: A Kindergarten for Future Play-goers (concerning a children's theater—children as actors in training, etc.—in connection with Education Alliance, East Side, New York City) - - The Theatre (June, 1907), pp. 154-156, X, XII, XIII.

Dramatization—B-Sixth Grade
April, 1907

KATE F. OSGOOD, Training Teacher

Student Teachers—
Grace Phelps, Ethel Sollinger, Pearl Thompson

PAUL REVERE'S RIDE

NOTE.—The appropriate part of Longfellow's poem is read to the audience before the play, and similarly appropriate parts at suitable times during scene shiftings.

ACT I.—The Midnight Alarm

Scene I.—The House of the Sexton of North Church

Characters:
    Paul Revere, the hero of the play.
    Robert Newman, the sexton of the church.
    Susan Newman, the sexton's wife.

[Old-fashioned kitchen of R. Newman's house. Big fire-place at one end of the room. Crane and kettles. Several high-back chairs. Spinning wheel in front of fire-place. Bellows hanging at one side of. fire-place. Curtain rises. Enter R. N.]

Mrs. N.: (Mr. N. hangs up his hat and coat and, blowing out his lantern, sets it down). Robert, you are later than usual. Have you heard any more news from the British?

Mr. N.: Nothing new. Things are about the same as they have been the last few days. There has been a stir among them, which looks a little suspicious.

Mrs. N.: I do wish those horrid red-coats would see that we Americans will not give up and so give us no more trouble. But I suppose there is no use thinking such good things and we must be prepared to meet the worst. (A loud knock at the door. Mrs. N. turns around with a startled look. Mr. N. opens the door and Paul Revere enters.)

Mr. N.: Why! Good evening, my friend! Any news?

Paul R.: Yes, I have just received this important message from Dr. Warren.

Mr. N. (breathlessly): Read! Read!

Paul R. (reading the note): Friend Revere—Just received word that the British are preparing to move, and we are very sure they are planning to capture our ammunition at Lexington and Concord. So you see Hancock and Adams will be in great danger. I will rely on your ability to help spread the alarm and warn these two men. Make immediate plans to leave the Charlestown shore at the moment we know more concerning the exact movements of the British. I have also informed Dawes to leave by the Boston Neck and help. Act according to your best judgment. Yours in haste, Joseph Warren.

(Burns the note.)

Mr. N.: There is no time to waste; immediate action must be taken.

Paul R.: I must go at once, for my men are waiting on the shore now to row me across to Charlestown where I can obtain a good swift horse.

Mr. N.: We must agree upon some signal so that you may know what route the British are going to take.

Paul R. (pondering): I have it! Hang one lantern in the belfry of the North Church if they go by land, and two if they go by sea. I will be on the opposite shore ready to spread the alarm. Goodwife, have the lanterns cleaned, and put fresh tallows in them. Good night! (Starts towards the door.)

Mr. and Mrs. N.: Good night!

Paul R.: May God speed you! (Exit Paul R. Curtain falls.)

Scene 2.—Near North Church

Characters:

Robert Newman.

Lieut. Col. Smith and British officers.

Major Pitcairn, a British officer.

British soldiers.

[Street scene. British barracks near by. R. Newman, walking up and down the street very quietly, suddenly, hearing voices, stops and listens. Recognizing the British, he steps aside. British soldiers, sitting around, talking and telling stories. Enter Lieut. Col. Smith. Officers and soldiers arise and salute him.]

Major P.: Attention! Fall in!

Lieut. Col. S. (speaking to the officers at one side) : I have. just received a message from Gen. Gage ordering us to march to Lexington and Concord to-night. Every one must move quietly, no drums must be beaten. Commands must be given in almost a whisper.

Officers (giving commands in low tones to the soldiers) : Forward! March! Left, right, left, right, etc.

(Exit soldiers and officers.)

[**Pantomime**—Robert Newman hanging the lantern in the tower. "Then he climbed," etc.]

ACT II.—Medford Town

Characters:

Timothy Belknap, Captain of the minute-men.

Hannah Belknap, Captain's wife.

Cynthia, Abigail, Sally, Nancy, Captain's daughters.

Timothy, Benjamin, Daniel, Ezekiel, Matthew, Captain's sons.

Paul Revere

Scene 1.—Street in front of Captain Belknap's House

[Clatter of horse's hoofs heard in the distance.]

Paul R.: Whoa! (Knocking loudly at the door and shouting.)

The Regulars are coming! Wake up! Rouse all the people! (Hannah B., with night-cap on her head, comes to the window.)

Hannah B. (calling loudly) : Mercy on us! What's the matter?

Paul R. (replying hurriedly) : Matter enough you'll find by daylight! The British are coming!

Capt. B. (coming to the window) : What's that! The Regulars are coming? Come in! I must have further particulars.

Paul R.: Very well, I will rest my horse for a few minutes.

(Curtain falls.)

Scene 2.—Interior of Captain Belknap's House

[Enter Capt. B., followed by Paul Revere.]

Paul R.: We must hasten. I have but a few minutes to spare.

Capt. B.: The whole country around must be notified. Here comes Timothy. Take old Dobbin and ride towards Lynn; notify everybody along the road and have them notify others. Zeke, you take Jerry and go towards Arlington.

Paul R.: Muster as many men as possible and take your stand here. Look out for the red-coats. There may be spies on the road. (Enter other members of the family one by one.) I just escaped capture at Charlestown Neck. (Exit Paul Revere.)

Mrs. B.: Girls, we must get busy and prepare plenty of food—gingerbread, doughnuts and hot coffee. Dan, you bring in a ham from the smoke-house.

Capt. B. (to the other two boys): Boys, we must get the powder and flints ready. (Enter neighbors and a general conversation follows. Curtain falls.)

ACT III.—Lexington

Scene 1.—Rev. Clarke's House

Characters:
  Jonas Clarke, minister.
  Anne Clarke, the minister's wife.
  John Hancock, Samuel Adams, Paul Revere, William
    Dawes, Sergeant Monroe, Dr. Prescott, and Guards.

[In front of Rev. Clarke's house. Sergeant Monroe and guards keeping watch. Clatter of horse's hoofs heard in the distance.]

Sergeant M.: Halt! Who goes there?

Paul R.: A messenger.

Sergeant M.: Be quiet! Make no noise! You'll wake up all the people in the house!

Paul R.: Noise! You'll have enough noise before morning. The red-coats are coming!

Rev. Clarke (appearing) : What's the trouble out here? (Seeing a stranger.) I can admit no strangers at this hour of the night.

J. Hancock (recognizing Paul Revere's voice, appears) : Come in Revere, we know you. Have you brought news from Dr. Warren?

Paul R.: Yes, Mr. Hancock, I was to warn you and Mr. Adams that the British, eight hundred strong, left Boston two hours before midnight with orders to capture and destroy the stores at Concord and were also to take you and Mr. Adams prisoners.

S. Adams (coming to the door) : Ah! They would give us quick passage to England, no doubt. But thanks to your timely warning, Revere, they will find that the birds have flown.

J. Hancock: I feel it my duty, Mr. Adams, to stay here and put myself at the head of the minute-men——

S. Adams (interrupting) : Your duty, as well as mine, is to work with the Provincial Committee of Safety. At present we are needed there. (Clatter of hoofs again heard. All listen as William Dawes approaches.)

All: Who is it? What is the news? Who are you?

Dawes: Dawes, with a message from Dr. Warren.

Paul R.: Ah! That is you, Dawes! I arrived but a short time since. You made quick time.

Dawes: I had several narrow escapes, but by strategy and the help of my faithful and wise old Dolly, we made our way through the British lines.

Paul R.: We must hasten if we would reach Concord before daylight.

Dr. Prescott: I will join you with your permission. I was delayed later than usual and have my horse here at the hitching post. Three chances are better than one.

Rev. Clarke: Yes, to be sure, spies are lurking about, no doubt. Some suspicious looking strangers were seen on the Concord road last week. (Exit Dawes, Prescott, and Paul Revere.)

Mrs. Clarke (in the meantime Mrs. C. has been busy preparing coffee and lunch, and comes to the door with coffee) : Come, gentlemen, you all need something refreshing before going.

You must drink a cup of coffee, whether you want anything to eat or not. (Exit Mrs. C.. She soon returns with a basket.) You must also take this basket of lunch that I have prepared. (Curtain falls.)

Scene 2.—Lexington

Characters:
Capt. Parker.
Thaddeus Bowman.
Major Pitcairn.
Minute-men, British soldiers.

[Lexington Common. Meeting-house in the background. Drum is heard. Muster of minute-men. Capt. Parker in command.]

Thad. B. (riding furiously up to the meeting-house): Here they come! Here are the British!

Capt. P. (orders the drum beat and gives command to form in line): The enemy is approaching! Remember the wishes of the Provincial Congress! "Stand your ground. Don't fire unless fired upon, but if they mean to have war, let it begin here." (All face the enemy as they approach.) We are outnumbered ten to one! We must retire!

Major P. (commands troops to halt and form line, facing the Americans): Disperse, you rebels! Lay down your arms! (Waves pistol in air.) You villians! Why don't you lay down your arms and disperse? (Soldiers fire a few scattering shots on each side, followed by a general discharge from the English. Fire is returned and war is begun. English cheer and retire towards Concord.)

ACT IV.—Concord Town

Scene 1.—Concord

Characters:
Col. Barrett, Dr. Prescott, Messenger.

[Groups of men, under command of Col. Barrett, concealing stores, musket balls, barrels of flour, beef, molasses, and candles. Talking as they work.]

Col. B.: 'Twas fortunate, Dr. Prescott, that `you made your escape and reached us as early as you did. Although we had received our first warning Sunday night, we certainly were not prepared for this sudden move. Were Revere and Dawes both captured?

Dr. Prescott: I think so. We were surrounded, but I managed to jump my horse over a stone wall and escaped——

Messenger: The red-coats are approaching! They are within two miles of the village.

Col. Barrett: We have no more time to conceal our stores. The rest we must defend. (Curtain falls.)

Scene 2.—Concord Bridge, Americans Defending

Characters:

Col. Barrett, Capt. Davis, Americans, British.

[Fifes and drums are heard as the Acton company approaches under command of Capt. Davis. Fifes play "White Cockade."]

Col. B. (looking toward Concord Town): They are setting fire to the stores we could not hide. We must force the bridge.

Capt. D.: Col. Barrett, we Acton minute-men crave your permission to clear the bridge. There is not a man in my company that is afraid.

Col. B.: Pass to the bridge without firing, but if fired upon, return the fire. It is the King's highway, and we have a right to march on it if we wish to go to Boston. Forward, march! (Tune of "White Cockade." On the bridge the English fire two distinct volleys. Men fall. Davis and others are either killed or wounded. Battle is on. English begin the retreat. Americans, approaching from every direction, drive the British toward Lexington. Curtain falls.)

Scene 3.—Pantomime

[Retreat. British soldiers, marching rapidly, are driven by ever increasing numbers in the rear and harassed on every side. Americans fire from behind stone walls and trees, retire and load, and so continue. Curtain falls.]

ACT V.—(Same as Act II.)

Scene 1.—Capt. Belknap's House (same scene as in Act II.)

Characters:
Same as in Act II.

[Mother and daughters anxiously awaiting the return of the father and sons.]

Cynthia: Don't worry so, mother. We feel sure that father and the boys are safe and will soon return.

Mother (looking from the window): Here comes Reuben now. (Reuben enters.) My son, have you seen anything of your father and the boys?

Reuben: Benjamin is coming down the road and the others will soon be here, I guess. What a chase we gave those lobster-backs!

Nancy: Goodwife Gerry says she heard our men drove them back along the Boston road on the double-quick. (Enter Capt. Belknap and Benjamin.)

Benjamin: Hurrah! Well, mother, girls, we won the victory after all. Those red-coats were in great confusion. Weren't used to our way of fighting.

Capt. B.: What a retreat that was! When they got back to Lexington their tongues were hanging out of their mouths like those of dogs after a chase. (Enter Ezekiel with head bound up.)

Mrs. Belknap: What is it, Ezekiel! Are you hurt?

Ezekiel: Only a scratch, mother. One of those red-coats thought he got his man. He made a pretty good shot, though.

Sally: Where are the red-coats now, father?

Capt. B.: Well, those who were not killed or wounded are probably now on Charlestown Neck.

Benjamin: 'Twas just at sunset, they entered Charlestown under the welcome shelter of the guns of Somerset.

Ezekiel: Yes, and not a moment too soon, for Col. Pickering with the Essex militia of seven hundred were within a quarter of a mile of them.

Benjamin: Had their road been blocked by these Essex men, they must have surrendered. (Enter Mrs. Brooks, a neighbor.)

Mrs. Brooks: Oh, Capt. Belknap, I hear drums beating down the Cambridge road. What does it mean?

Capt. B.: More minute-men coming from distant towns. There are twenty thousand of them in Massachusetts alone. By to-morrow there'll be militia here from Rhode Island, Connecticut, and New Hampshire.

Reuben: War has really begun. But, father, I fear we shall come short of powder and bullets.

Capt. B. and Boys: Yes, I fear that too.

Mrs. Brooks: We must melt up all our pewter platters, bowls and plates and run them into bullets.

Mrs. Belknap: Take all the pewter dishes you want, girls, but the thought of the terrible days to come is almost too much for me.

Capt. B.: Yes, there are hard days, perhaps years of struggle before us, but do not grieve, Deborah, for our cause is a just one and we must succeed.

Mrs. Belknap: Yes, we may succeed. But, oh, will the day ever come when troubles like these will be settled without this cruel fighting and awful bloodshed!

(Curtain falls.)

The Court of King Cole

The Frogs and the Brownies

The Signing of the Compact in the Cabin of the Mayflower

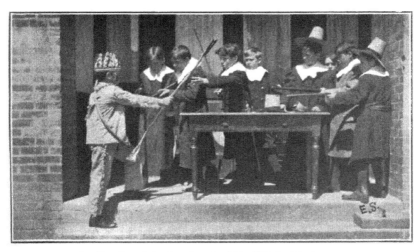

The Receipt of the Rattlesnake Skin Filled with Arrows

The Knighting of Galahad

Starting on the Quest